© 2021 Keisha McDonald, MS, MA, LPC, NCC

ISBN:978-1-955234-14-6

For permission requests, contact Keisha McDonald at amourlegacipublishing@gmail.com.

This is a work of fiction. Any resemblance to actual events or persons, living or dead, is entirely coincidental.

1st editionBook Design: Keisha McDonald

Production: AmourLegaci Publishing

Editing: Keisha McDonald

Illustration: Keisha McDonald

Publisher: AmourLegaci Publishing

To order: Amazon.com, www.barnesandnoble.com

Author Website:Amourlegacipublishing.com

Printed in United States of America

What is a comma?

a punctuation mark (,) indicating a _pause_ between parts of a sentence

Why a comma?

to remind you to pause and take a moment for YOU

When you take a moment and <u>pause</u>, you have time to think of what to do next...

 PAUSE, I AM NOT MY ANXIETY

What's anxiety?

 Anxiety is when you feel nervous, overwhelmed, worried or anxious

Some physical symptoms of what you may *feel* is emotion overload, muscle tension, headache, dizziness, shakes, heart racing and rapid breathing.

why do I get anxiety?

We all have anxiety but when hard things happen to you it makes you feel a lot of different emotions

When do I get anxiety?

You get anxiety when you are in uncomfortable situations, talking about uncomfortable things, before a test, when you are scared or sad

But....
there are many
things you can
do to help your
anxiety

GO AWAY

do I get rid of
my anxiety?

Grounding

what is that?

Grounding is a technique that helps you focus on where you are right now!

Active Grounding Countdown Method

NAME
5
things you

NAME
4
things you

NAME
3
things you

NAME
2
things you

NAME
1
thing you

See

feel

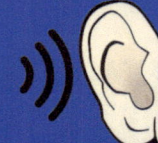
hear

smell

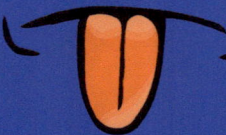
taste

Active Grounding
Colors & Shapes Method

Step #1:   Pick 1 color

Step #2:   Name everything in the room that is that color

Step #3:   Pick a 2nd color

Step #4:   Name everything in the room that is that color

Step #5:   Pick a 3rd color

Step #6:   Name everything in the room that is that color

Step #7:   Pick 1 shape

Step #8:   Name everything in the room that is that shape

Now try a coping skill   ⇨

Mindfulness is a type of meditation where you focus on being aware of what you're sensing and feeling right now, without interpretation or judgment.

Practicing mindfulness involves breathing methods, guided imagery, and other methods to relax the body and mind

Guided imagery is focusing your imagination to create calm, peaceful images in your mind, providing a "mental escape."

Breathing Techniques

Breathing techniques are used for mindfulness, coping skills, grounding and self care. Regulating our breathing helps to calm our bodies down.

Triangle Breathing

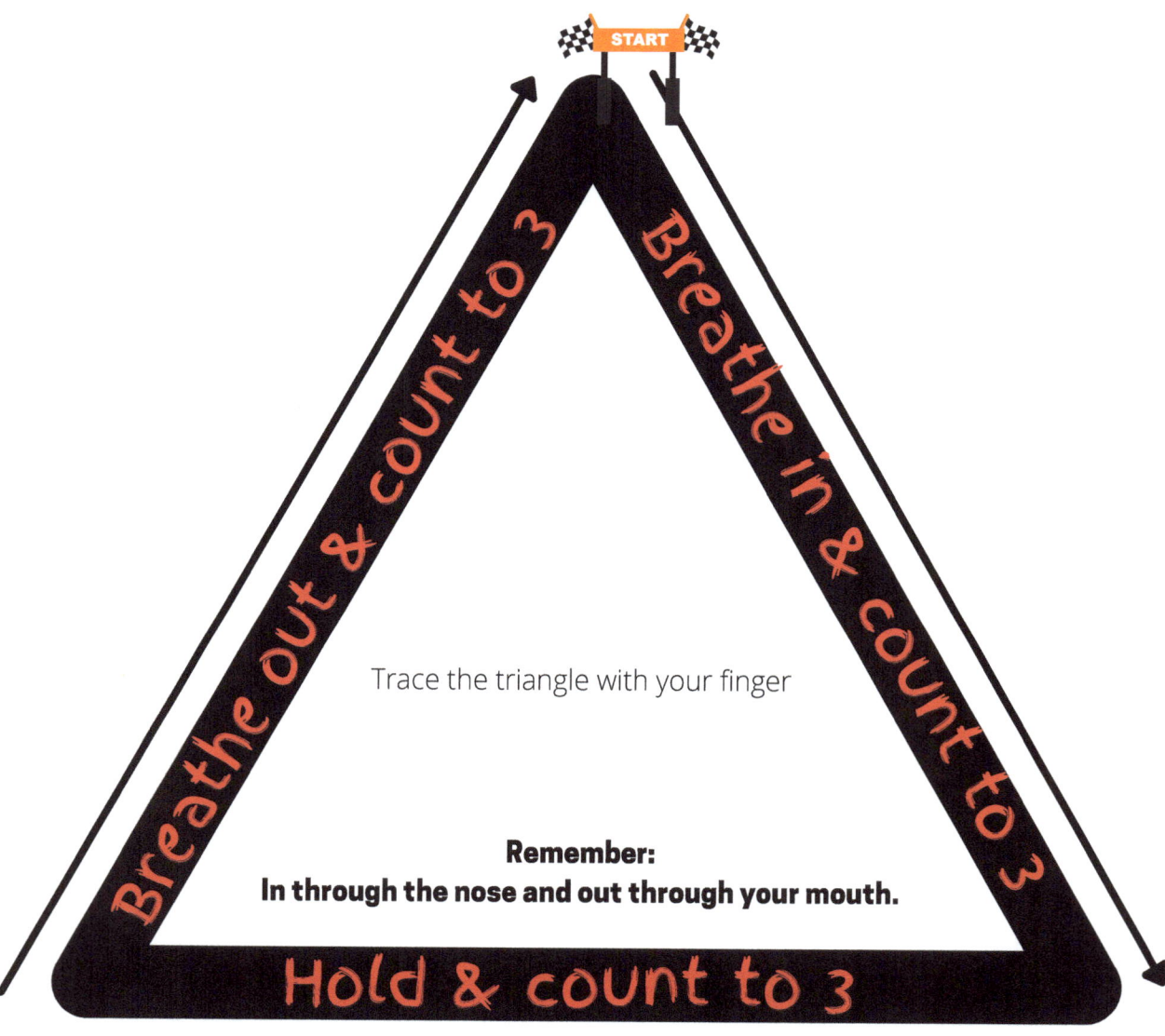

START

Breathe in & count to 3

Breathe out & count to 3

Trace the triangle with your finger

Remember:
In through the nose and out through your mouth.

Hold & count to 3

As you breathe in you breathe in stating I am feeling calm you breathe out stating I am releasing my anxiety you breathe in new energy you breathe out releasing worries

Square Breathing

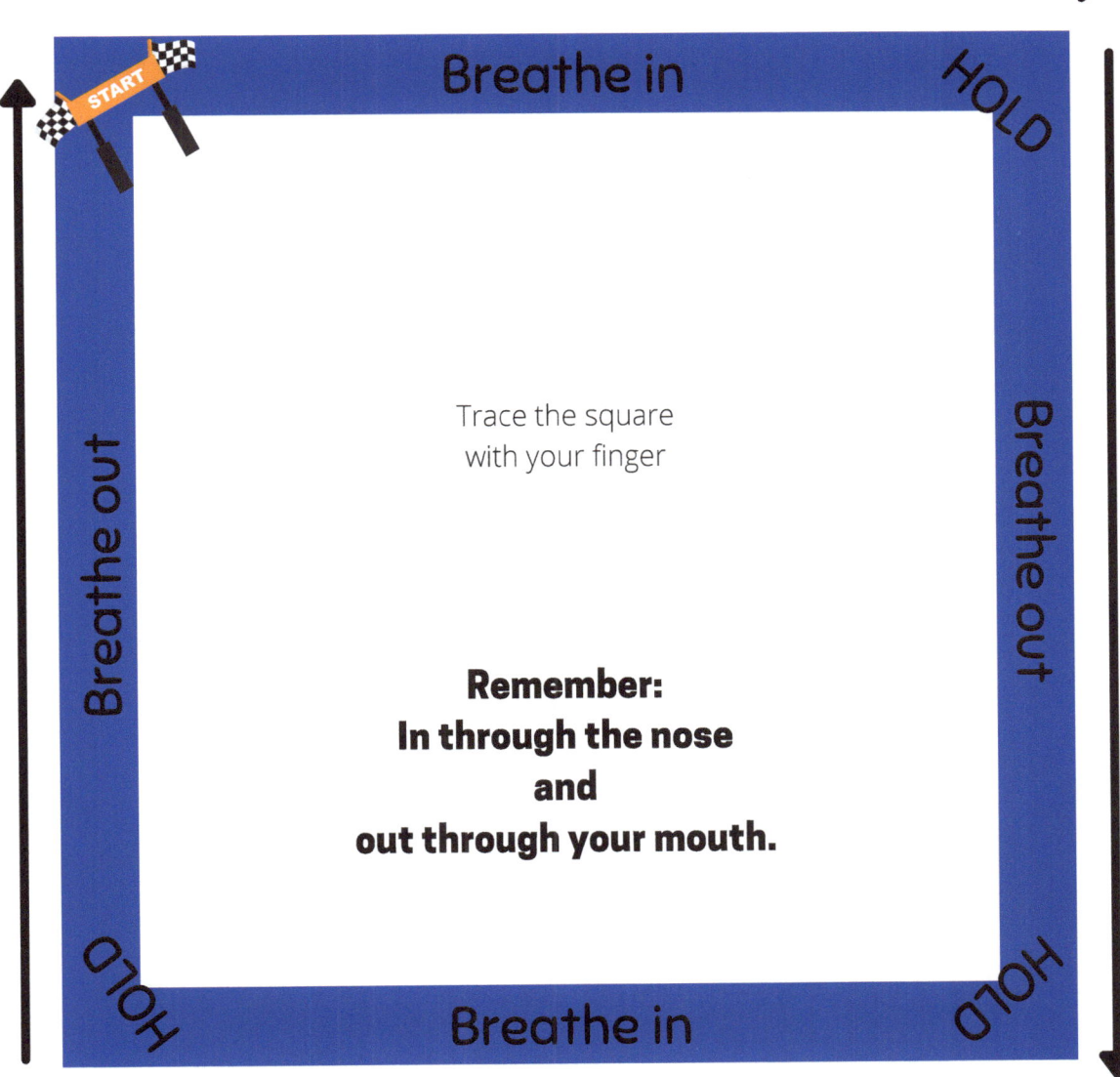

As you breathe in you breathe in stating I am feeling calm you breathe out stating I am releasing my anxiety you breathe in new energy you breathe out releasing worries

Infinity Breathing

Trace the infinity with your finger

Remember:
In through the nose
and
out through your mouth.

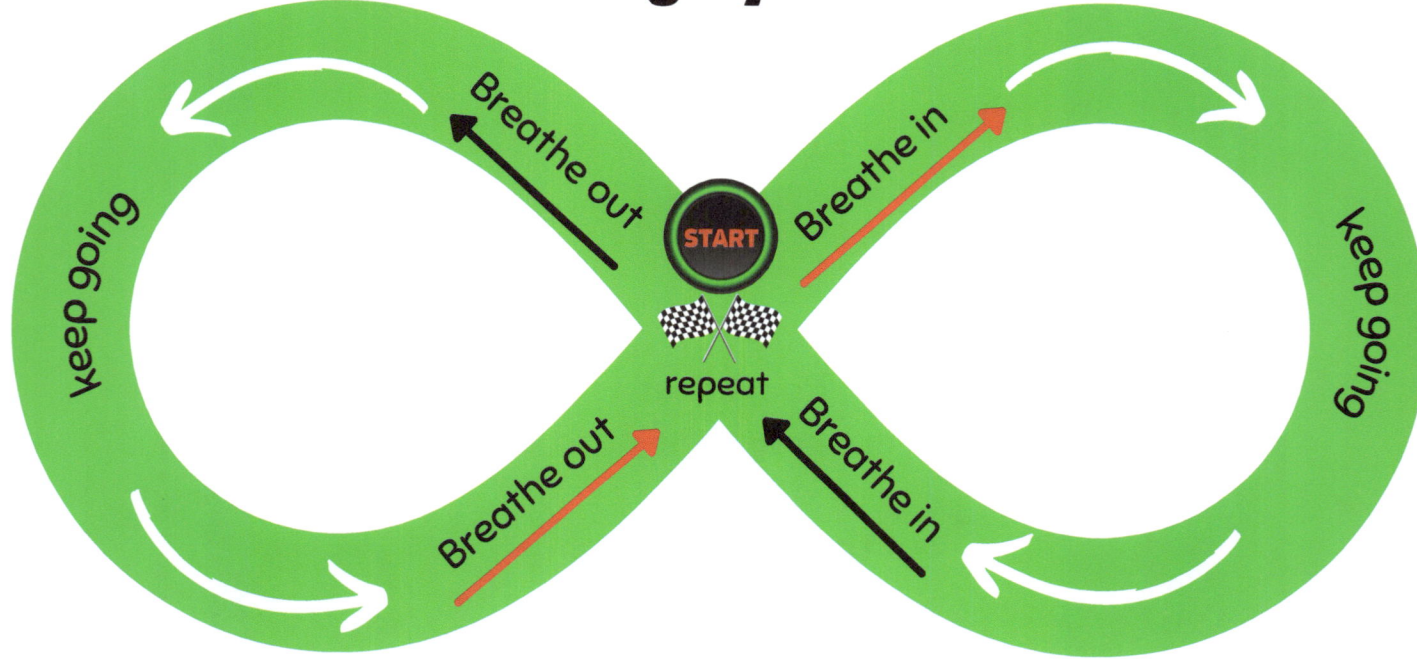

As you breathe in you breathe in
stating I am feeling calm
you breathe out stating I am releasing my anxiety
you breathe in new energy
you breathe out releasing worries

NEXT UP...

Coping skills

Coping skills are things that help you manage and distracts you from the hard stuff.

Drawing

is coping......
drawing a picture
of the people and things
that make you feel safe.

Listening to music is coping

Watching your favorite TV show is coping

Stress Jar

Watching my stress jar or taking a walk helps anxiety go away.

YOU CAN DO IT!

You can make your own jar later. Check out the instructions in the back of the book!!

Affirmations

Things to tell yourself
and keep telling yourself

YOU ARE AMAZING

you are ENOUGH

I LOVE ME

DO IT FOR YOURSELF

DON'T QUIT

Believe IN yourself

YOU matter

Self Care

SELF ♡ CARE

Self care is a very important part of regulating emotions.

ME TIME

Eating comfort food is self care

Journaling is a part of self care and coping

Self care is taking
a break or a nap.

Self care is making a bracelet to remind you to ground yourself.

Smell essential oils to help anxiety go away

Now you have the tools to help your anxiety go away!

1. Grounding/Mindfulness
2. Coping
3. Selfcare

How will your anxiety go away?

Remember:

You are not your anxiety

Therapy Activity corner:

Take some time and discuss when the child feels anxiety.
Have the child write down some things they can do to cope with these feelings when they are happening.

Make a plan for what to do when these feelings are happening.

Ask the child what they need at that time?

What are your needs?

HOW A GLITTER JAR CAN HELP KIDS CONTROL THEIR FEELINGS

When kids are stressed, sad, or angry, the amygdala's natural fight, flight, or freeze response kicks in, making rational decision-making nearly impossible.

Mindfulness gives kids space and time to calm down and pay attention to what is going on in their body and environment. Regularly practicing mindfulness reduces stress and increases wellness and self-control.

Glitter jars are a useful mindfulness tool at home and school. Watching the glitter swirl to the bottom of the jar gives kids time to calm down and regain control.

Instructions

Pour 1/2 cup of distilled warm water into the jar.
Pour 1/2 cup of glitter glue or clear glue into the jar.
Add 1-2 teaspoons of extra glitter, beads or buttons to the jar.
Fill up the remainder of the jar with warm distilled water.
If desired, use a hot glue gun to squeeze a ring of glue around the lid of the jar.
You can also use small plastic jars from dollar store.

Resources

In case of emergency, please go to your nearest hospital or contact your therapist or find one @

Psychology Today

If you are struggling with thoughts of harming yourself please talk to someone or call National Suicide Prevention Lifeline
Hours: Available 24 hours. Languages: English, Spanish.

References

Mindfulness, pg. 19, Retrieved from https://www.mayoclinic.org/healthy-lifestyle/consumer-health/in-depth/mindfulness-exercises/art-20046356

Guided imagery, pg. 20. Retrieved from https://my.clevelandclinic.org/departments/wellness/integrative/treatments-services/guided-imagery

About the Author

Keisha McDonald is a Grand Rapids, Michigan native, a mother of four and Banena (Grandmother) to 2. She holds a double Master's degree in Psychology and Clinical Mental Health Counseling and is a practicing Limited Licensed Professional Counselor. She has fostered children for over 10 years and adopted 2. Combined with her passion for helping kids and education, through her books she has been prompted to help children with fostering the self esteem to know they are not alone.

www.ingramcontent.com/pod-product-compliance
Lightning Source LLC
Chambersburg PA
CBHW041434120626
46547CB00002B/209